Original title:
What's the Point of All This?

Copyright © 2025 Creative Arts Management OÜ
All rights reserved.

Author: Zachary Prescott
ISBN HARDBACK: 978-1-80566-196-2
ISBN PAPERBACK: 978-1-80566-491-8

The Lament of a Wandering Soul

I wandered through a crowded street,
With socks that don't quite match my feet.
I stopped to ask a wise old cat,
"What's the deal with all this chit-chat?"

He stared and said, "You silly freak,
Life's a game, but who's to speak?
Chase the fish, ignore the fowl,
Just find joy in this lost howl!"

In cafés, people sip their brew,
While pondering what they should pursue.
A muffin waved and said with cheer,
"Just eat me quick, let go of fear!"

Yet here I roam, with thoughts so wild,
Like a puppy chasing after a child.
But laughter bubbles, fills the void,
Amidst the chaos, I'm overjoyed!

Stories Yet to Be Told

In a cupboard, dust bunnies dance,
With tales of crumbs and a lost romance.
A teapot giggles, steaming with pride,
"We brew the best of thoughts inside!"

Grandpa's stories fit for a throne,
Like socks he loses, not much to own.
But listen closely, dear little sprites,
His tales can light up the longest nights.

The dog on the porch, he snores like a bear,
Dreaming of dragons or perhaps a hare.
"Don't take life too seriously," he yawns,
"Grab a snack, enjoy all the dawns!"

So here we sit, with snacks in our lap,
Reading the tales that life's but a quap.
With laughs as our compass, we drift along,
Creating a world where we all belong!

Stars Aligned

In the cosmos, the stars all meet,
With cosmic jokes, they dance on heat.
You ponder deep, as comets play,
While aliens giggle and drift away.

The moon winks slyly, a cheeky sprite,
Saying life's just a big ol' flight.
Catch a ride on a shooting star,
But watch your seatbelt, oh so far!

Questions Unearthed

Digging deep in the sandy beach,
Finding questions they seldom teach.
Why do socks vanish in thin air?
Aliens likely took my spare!

With shovels and buckets, we gather dust,
Is it for answers? Or just for fun? We must.
Gazing at grains that twinkle like gold,
The mysteries are there, but really, so bold!

Flickering Flames of Uncertainty

A candle flickers, its shadow plays,
While I sit, lost in the haze.
Fire's a friend, yet a tricky foe,
Will it roast marshmallows or start a show?

The flames dance wild, a twirling spree,
As I munch on popcorn, just me and me.
Will the light guide or hide away?
Who knows what tomorrow may say?

The Landscapes of Longing

In fields of dreams, we skip and hop,
Chasing rainbows, we giggle and stop.
But what's that itch just out of reach?
It's probably just a lesson to teach!

With clouds of whims, we float along,
Serenading choices with a silly song.
Do we pick the right path or just roam?
It's like finding Gucci in a thrift store's home!

A Prelude to the Unknown

The curtain rises, the lights go dim,
It's not a mystery, it's more like a whim.
Characters shuffle, then strike a pose,
In this grand play, anything goes!

With popcorn ready and drinks in hand,
Will I find answers, a life unplanned?
Or just laugh at the wonderful mess,
As life unfolds in a quirky dress?

Eclipsed by Questions

Why do we speed while life crawls slow?
Each tick of the clock whispers, 'Whoa!'
We ponder the stars in the vast night sky,
While debating the merits of pizza pie.

Do chickens have thoughts? Is the sky really blue?
Or is it a scheme from the cows we knew?
As we rubberneck at life's strange parade,
We giggle at wonders, our minds unafraid.

The Weight of Unanswered Thoughts

In a world of questions, we tread so light,
Avoiding the burdens that drag us from sight.
Is gravity real, or just a bad prank?
Why can't I find where all my socks sank?

We ponder existence like it's a quiz,
Yet laugh at the thought that nobody knows this.
Caught in a web of confounding thoughts,
We skip like a stone, revenge on our knots.

Fragments of Purpose

What is the meaning of a lost sock's plight?
Could it be hiding, shining so bright?
Each puzzle piece scattered, no picture in view,
Yet we search for the answers like detectives do.

Is dinner still dinner if we eat it at noon?
Are there monsters that laugh, out-dancing the moon?
In the chaos of life, absurdity reigns,
And we chuckle at logic that it never attains.

The Path Without a Signpost

Wandering whims on this puzzling trail,
Where questions roam free and answers go stale.
Are we all just ducks in a giant parade?
Or is life a joke that we've all overstayed?

With each twist and turn, we're lost in delight,
Like squirrels on a quest in the dark of the night.
So we laugh, and we ponder this riddle divine,
As we trip over thoughts and embrace the benign.

When Stars Refuse to Shine

The stars are tired, they took a break,
They left us wondering, make no mistake.
The moon's on the couch, binge-watching a show,
While here on the ground, we're lost in the glow.

A comet just sneezed, and scattered the night,
If space is a puzzle, where's the flashlight?
We search for answers but find only quips,
And laugh at the cosmos, while practicing flips.

In the Absence of Clarity

In foggy thoughts, we dance a jig,
Confusion swirls, oh what a gig!
Like trying to juggle jellybeans,
We grasp for meaning in silly scenes.

The roadmap's missing, we're lost in cheer,
Does it matter? Maybe, or it's just a dear.
With questions echoing like old jokes told,
We chuckle and ponder, bold and uncontrolled.

The Maze of Ambiguity

In a maze of twists, we run in place,
Chasing our tails in a dizzying race.
The walls are closing, the cheese is a myth,
Still, we laugh as we trip, ignoring the rift.

Directions unclear, but spirits are bright,
Why find an exit, when you could take flight?
With each wrong turn, a giggle we earn,
In this wacky world, there's so much to learn.

Chronicles of a Wandering Heart

My heart's on a journey, a train with no tracks,
It skips and it hops, never looking back.
Each stop along the way is a curious sight,
With tacos and laughter, oh what a delight!

It wanders through rainbows, then slips in a puddle,
While pondering wisdom, it finds some trouble.
Each laugh shakes its core, each chuckle a spark,
A dance in the moonlight, a stroll in the dark.

The Puzzle of the Unsolved

Life's a jigsaw, pieces stray,
Finding corners leads the way.
Sometimes flipped, and upside down,
Where's the edge? Lost in the town.

Questions linger, yet we smile,
Life's a riddle, stay awhile.
Who needs answers? Just some fun,
Puzzles thrive 'til day is done.

Capturing Fragments of the Present

Snap a pic, it's just a blur,
Moments fly, like bees that stir.
Captured laughter, fleeting winks,
What's life about? Who even thinks?

Fragments stolen through the lens,
Collecting smiles like old friends.
Each snapshot's worth a thousand words,
Except for when it's all absurd.

A Symphony of Sighs

Oh what a tune, the sighs we sing,
Composing chaos, our favorite fling.
Life's notes are sharp, sometimes quite flat,
Yet here we are, imagine that!

Harmony in everyday plight,
Dancing awkwardly, what a sight!
Tiresome tunes, yet we all sway,
Sighs composed in a cheeky way.

The Dance of Shadows and Light

Shadows stretch, then twist and twirl,
Playing hide-and-seek in a whirl.
Sunlight giggles through the leaves,
While shadows plot, oh how it deceives!

Dance around, life's silly play,
Light hearted as we drift away.
Each step a chuckle, a funny twist,
In this dance, who can resist?

Fleeting Shadows of Tomorrow

Here we dance on dreams like sand,
Chasing grains that slip through hand.
With each laugh, we spin around,
Yet where we land, we've never found.

Ticking clocks and silly hats,
Waltzing with the chubby cats.
In the mirror, a jesting face,
Searching for the missing trace.

We giggle at the world so wide,
Riding waves on joy's own tide.
But peek behind the curtain's veil,
And witness humor's grand regale.

So toast to shadows, fleeting friends,
Each moment a twist that never ends.
Life's a joke that's never told,
In the punchline, brave and bold.

Chasing the Elusive Why

Why did the chicken cross the street?
To find more questions, quite a feat.
It clucked and giggled, wings askew,
With a purpose that nobody knew.

In a world of ponder and dilemma,
Happiness floats like a rare stemma.
Searching under socks and shoes,
For answers mixed in colors, hues.

We ponder, muse, and nod our heads,
Chasing thoughts like lively threads.
In the chase, we find delight,
But the why might just take flight.

So let's laugh at riddles and puns,
And ride along like joyful runs.
In the midst of puzzled sighs,
We find our bliss in silly whys.

In the Labyrinth of Purpose

Labyrinthine paths of thought,
Twisting lives we never sought.
With each corner, laughter swells,
As we trip on our own spells.

The minotaur, he grins and laughs,
Chasing dreams through tangled paths.
With a snack in each great hand,
We wander lost in this strange land.

Maps are drawn with crayon charms,
Leading us to silly farms.
Where cabbage dances, and peas sing tunes,
Under the glow of merry moons.

Let's lose ourselves in this maze,
Finding joy in funny ways.
Purpose hides in mirthful guise,
Where laughter is the greatest prize.

Fragmented Reflections on a Glassy Sea

On a sea so smooth, we stand,
Gazing deep with grains of sand.
Reflections twist like jellyfish,
With each ripple, a fleeting wish.

We toss our doubts like stones ashore,
Counting waves that ask for more.
A funny fish passes by,
Wearing spectacles, oh my, oh my!

Fragmented thoughts float on the tide,
In every splash, strange truths abide.
Life is but a quirky tale,
Where logic sometimes starts to fail.

So laugh as mirrors break and bend,
In absurdity, we find a friend.
On this glassy sea, we sail, with glee,
Finding treasures in the mystery.

Whispers in the Void

In the dark, I hear a sound,
A chuckle echoing all around.
Is it my brain or just a breeze?
Maybe life's just here to tease.

I ask my cat, she gives a stare,
As if she knows what's truly fair.
I sip my tea, it spills a bit,
Life's a game, I can't submit.

The mailbox gives a muted cheer,
Another bill? Ah, what a year!
Floating thoughts like dandelion seeds,
In the wind, where chaos leads.

So here I sit, with socks astray,
Laughing loud at life's grand play.
For in this sprawl, with wiggles free,
We dance around absurdity.

The Dance of Aimlessness

Life's a party with no real theme,
A conga line on a broken beam.
I trip and fall, I laugh and twirl,
Every stumble, the world's a whirl.

Chasing clouds that drift and sway,
I ponder long on light's ballet.
The sun just giggles all the time,
As I compose this silly rhyme.

In the fridge, a moldy peach,
Reminds me life's a crazy speech.
We wobble here, we wobble there,
And dance like no one really cares.

So grab your hat and don those shoes,
Let's break the rules and share our blues.
For in this jest we find delight,
A wobbly journey feels just right.

Threads of Existence

Stitching life with threads of joy,
A tangled mess like a kid's toy.
Knots of worries, strings of hope,
Interwoven in a slippery slope.

I found a sock, mismatched and torn,
In the drawer where dreams are worn.
It told me stories of days gone by,
In a voice like a soft sigh.

The coffee pot hums a tune so sweet,
While the toast ejects like it's on repeat.
"Oh what fun!" I shout aloud,
To my empty chair, so proud.

So let's weave laughter through the strands,
With silly puns and messy hands.
In this tapestry, we find our place,
A whimsical, chaotic embrace.

Chasing Fleeting Grains

In the hourglass, grains slip through,
Like tiny whispers—who knew?
Each one giggles as it falls,
Life's a riddle with silly calls.

I ran to catch them, wind at back,
Only to trip, what a knack!
The universe just rolled its eyes,
As I fumbled, aiming for the skies.

A squirrel chuckles up a tree,
"Why worry, mate? Just let it be!"
And I think, in this grand spree,
Chasing grains isn't up to me.

So I lie back on grassy greens,
And watch the clouds in shredded scenes.
For in this chase, I find the jest,
Life's just a game, and I'm a guest.

The Fleeting Nature of a Whisper

A whisper danced through the air,
Like a butterfly trapped in a stare.
We chase it down, but oh so sly,
It flutters away, and we just sigh.

Around the room it twirls and dips,
Tickling our ears like sweet little quips.
We ponder its purpose, its reason to flutter,
While mopping up crumbs from our peanut-butter.

But data proves, as I take a guess,
Even a whisper can cause quite a mess.
So laugh it off, don't take it too hard,
A soft little chuckle, your own safety guard.

In the Heart of Uncertainty

Am I here or simply a ghost?
Daydreaming while I nibble my toast?
The toaster pops, but I look away,
Did I make it clear? I hope it won't stray.

The clock ticks loud, will it ever stop?
Like socks without partners, they dance and swap.
Building castles out of stale old bread,
While pondering if I'm better off dead.

So here's to the slips and the falls, my friend,
To questions that dangle, like a loose, wild end.
We shrug at the nonsense; revel in glee,
In this grand comedy, who needs a decree?

Unfolding Layers of Existence

Life's a lasagna, all layered and stacked,
Each noodle carefully, and slightly whacked.
The sauce spills over; the cheese has a say,
While the garlic bread whispers, 'Hey, let's play!'

We scoop up our plates, but wait—what's this?
A mystery meatball wrapped up in bliss.
I ponder its origins, its purpose unclear,
While the salad just laughs, 'This is my year!'

So fork at the ready, let's dive on in,
With jokes on the table, let the party begin.
Life's just a banquet, odd flavors combined,
Feast on the laughter; it's truly sublime.

Chasing Echoes of Yesterday's Sun

The sun set low, a clown in disguise,
Waving goodbye with its bright orange fries.
As shadows now dance with a giggle and twirl,
I chase after memories, oh what a whirl!

Through puddles of laughter, where dreams take their run,

They splash in the moonlight; it's all just good fun.
But wait, what was that? A flicker, a glint,
Did yesterday's sun forget to leave a hint?

So onward I bounce to the beat of my heart,
Each echo a puzzle, a fragmented art.
With jokes in my pocket and hope on my sleeve,
Tomorrow's bright sunlight, in laughter, I believe.

Unraveled Knots of Ambition

Tangled threads in a grand old dream,
Chasing tails like a dog on cream.
We climb the heights with shoes untied,
Who needs a map? Just enjoy the ride.

Plans collide in a dance so bold,
As laughter echoes in stories told.
Yet here we are, with wild schemes,
Just bickering over ice cream dreams.

Spinning wheels with glee and flair,
Who knew ambition could lead to despair?
A juggling act on a trampoline,
It's all a circus, behind the scene.

So let's toast to chaotic paths,
Where nothing's clear, yet always laughs.
In this mess we call our quest,
We find the fun and call it the best.

The Allure of the Unknown

Peering through the fog, what's out there?
A dancing shadow, without a care.
We wear our capes and strike a pose,
In quest for treasure, who really knows?

Bump into giants or stumble on mice,
Each day's a gamble, roll the dice.
A treasure map scribbled on the back,
But oops! We lost it, instead we snack.

Chasing whispers of ghosts and ghouls,
Life's a puzzle, but where are the tools?
We laugh at the strange, the wild, the new,
Pretending we're lost, but really, who knew?

In the end, it's the stories spun,
Of mysterious roads and impromptu fun.
So let's wander where the wild winds blow,
With a wink in our eyes, let's steal the show.

Mosaics of the Mind's Eye

Pieces scattered, vibrant and bright,
A jigsaw puzzle, what a sight!
Each color tells its own little tale,
But where's the corner piece? Oh, it's gone pale!

Dreams are splattered like paint on the wall,
Mixed up visions that trip and fall.
We tilt our heads, squinting to see,
Is that a dragon or just my tea?

Thoughts bounce around like balls in a pin,
Creating chaos that grows from within.
We wear our quirks like a badge of pride,
No map required, we'll just take a ride.

So here's to the mess that makes us whole,
To the zany journey, that's the goal.
In this gallery of jumbled delight,
We find our humor, our spark, our light.

Following the Footprints of Fable

Once upon a time, or so they say,
We chased the clouds like kids at play.
With every tale spun, so grand and tall,
We slip on tales stuck to the wall.

Footprints lead us, some big, some small,
To dragons, fairies, and funny balls.
But who wrote the script? No one can tell,
Except the cat, who just knows it well.

In the woods of wonder, we dance with glee,
Echoing laughter from far and free.
Between the lines of a storybook,
We find our giggles and forbidden nook.

So let our fables twist and bend,
With each new chapter, laughter to lend.
In this merry chase, we'll joyfully roam,
For every story leads us back home.

Waiting for a Whisper

I sat and stared at my empty cup,
The coffee left, like my will to sup.
I pondered deep, with a furrowed brow,
While my cat plotted in silence, somehow.

An email pinged, my heart took flight,
It was just a coupon—oh, what a sight!
I laughed at the absurdity of it all,
Waiting for wisdom, but a cashback call!

Each day I search for signs from fate,
But I mostly just find my lost mate.
My phone buzzes with trivial noise,
While I ponder my life with old toys.

In the grand scheme, am I on track?
Or just chasing my tail, a goofy quack?
But hey, if laughter is life's true sense,
I'll settle for giggles and lame recompense!

The Quest for Elusive Answers

I grabbed a map, set out for the truth,
But all I found was a missing tooth.
A squirrel scolded as I wandered vast,
Was my quest too serious? Am I not a blast?

I hiked through fog, asking trees for advice,
But they just rustled, not even polite.
A sign appeared, it read 'Not today,'
Am I chasing shadows? Oh, what a display!

My friend says life's like a box of fries,
You gotta dip deep, but oil so flies!
With each crunchy bite, I mull and chew,
Searching for meanings like a cook seeking stew.

So here I sit, with ketchup in hand,
Reflecting on queries both random and grand.
Maybe the answers fit snug if we play,
With a playful heart, we'll dance through the day!

Amidst the Echoes of Indifference

In crowded rooms, I shout my name,
But echoes laugh, playing a silly game.
I wear a sombrero to stand out clear,
Yet folks just nod, lost in their beer.

I tell a joke, but it falls flat,
The crickets speak up, 'That's just your cat!'
I search for relevance in the everyday,
While socks on my feet choose to disobey.

The world spins on with a shrug and a grin,
As I ponder where my journey begins.
Shall I climb mountains or stick to the ground?
With laughs so silly, life's joy can be found.

So dance to the echoes, laugh at the plight,
In the realm of indifference, we find our light.
Though questions linger like fog in the air,
We'll weave through the nonsense, with nary a care!

The Search for Meaning in the Mundane

I woke up to dishes piled high as a hill,
In search of meaning, oh what a thrill!
My toaster popped up like a surprise attack,
A bread slice flying, down to my snack!

The mailman arrived, with bills like a sport,
All I wanted was a letter, or report.
I wandered outside, the grass tickled my toes,
"Is there meaning here?" the answer just shows.

A ladybug danced on my pet rock's head,
I wished for wisdom, but lost it instead.
The sun tickled leaves with laughter and light,
'Find joy in the mundane,' it seemed to recite.

So here's to the simple, the silly, the small,
With each quirky moment, we're having a ball!
In the dance of existence, let humor unfold,
For the mundane's the canvas, where stories are told!

Shadows Dance on the Wall

Shadows stretch, silly leaps,
A cat rehearses, a laugh peeps.
Chasing toes with determined grace,
What's the goal? Just a playful race.

Silhouette parties, laughter rings,
As the toaster unexpectedly sings.
Why ponder deep when fun's in sight?
Burnt toast or not, it feels so right.

The light flickers, moods go wild,
Hopping about like a jolly child.
In this dance of goofs and grins,
Is it worth it? All the wins!

So let's twirl and spin anew,
Forget the why, let's just pursue.
For shadows, like friends, will always play,
In this kooky light, we find our way.

Intersections of Now and Never

At the corner of Worry and Fun,
A signposts saying 'You've just begun'.
Traffic lights blink, but who obeys?
Detours lead to the silliest stays.

There's a squirrel directing the show,
In a bow tie made from a potato!
Follow the path of banana peels,
Where the humor just zealously squeals.

Lost in the maze of 'What do I do?',
A map with doodles, a brave kangaroo.
Here's where chaos makes all the sense,
Trading logic for moments intense.

So when you're stuck at that odd crossroad,
Remember: laughter is an awesome code.
In the intersections, joy seeks to thrive,
And you just might feel vividly alive.

Dreams That Never Sleep

Dreams fluffy like clouds, they swirl and hop,
Through a carnival where night won't stop.
A poodle in pajamas takes to the sky,
While unicorns giggle, oh my, oh my!

They weave through stars with sprinkle dust,
Making a wish is an absolute must.
Naps are for kittens, not silly souls,
Here dreams ignite like outrageous goals.

Never a dull moment in sleepy town,
Where proposals to dance leave no one down.
Chasing moonbeams, we giggle and spin,
The night is young, let the fun begin!

So let's tiptoe softly through slumber's door,
Where dreams that never sleep, implore.
For what's more silly than giggling wide?
In a world where oddities coincide.

The Threads That Connect Us

Threads of laughter weave through the air,
Connecting souls with a fabulous flair.
Tangled yarn balls, curious cats,
Making a mess of cozy chats.

A stitch of kindness, a seam of cheer,
Crafting community, far and near.
From pie on the windowsill, deliciously sweet,
To band-aids for hearts—let's not miss a beat!

In this tapestry where quirks unite,
We find shared stories that feel so right.
Knots of joy, a flip-flop parade,
Together we dance, our worries will fade.

So grab that thread, let's laugh in sync,
Life's a quirky quilt—so don't you think?
In the fabric of fun that we spin each day,
The ties that bind us, all find a way.

Spectres of a Lost Season

Leaves once danced, now taking flight,
They whisper secrets, dimmed by night.
Ghosts of summer, they laugh and play,
Where did the sun go, who can say?

Mittens missing, socks have fled,
Chasing autumn, dreams we've shed.
Pumpkins roll like wayward balls,
Spooking us with their goofy calls.

Frogs in raincoats, all confused,
Wondering why they feel misused.
Mice in hats and cats on skates,
Life's a circus; let's call it fate.

And somehow through this silly strife,
We find a chuckle in this life.
So raise a glass, toast with laughter,
To seasons lost and ghosts we're after!

Eclipsed Horizons and Hidden Truths

Under moons that wink and fade,
Shadows mingle, plans are laid.
Stars are giggling, hidden bright,
Do they know the joke tonight?

Tea leaves swirling, fortunes told,
Cards of fortune green and bold.
Yet here we sit, all puzzled out,
Finding answers we can't shout.

Cows in glasses, floating by,
Pondering truths as they fly high.
Mirrors crack with giggles loud,
Who's the fairest? That's the crowd!

But even as we spin our tales,
Life's a series of whimsical fail.
So dance your dance, you quirky soul,
In this odd game, you're on a roll!

A Voyage Into the Uncharted

Sails are flapping, winds a'howlin',
Maps are crumpled, minds are growlin'.
What's that there? An island? No!
Just the cat in a funny pose.

Navigating through sock-filled seas,
Cannonballs made of sneezy cheese.
Pirates chuckle and shake their heads,
While mermaids dream of cozy beds.

Crabs recite Shakespeare in the sand,
Wishing on stars, takes a brave hand.
As waves recede, all's quite absurd,
Who knew the ocean was so well-versed?

With laughter as our guiding star,
We chart our course, wherever we are.
So let's set sail, no need for maps,
Just embrace the bumps and joyful claps!

Pebbles in the Stream of Life

Tiny pebbles, each one a story,
Rolling through the stream in glory.
Splashing water, giggling stones,
Who knew life had such funny tones?

Frogs wear ties, frogs wear glee,
Jumping over clichés we see.
"Why so serious?" they croak with pride,
As they flip and flop, what a ride!

Fish with sunglasses swim around,
Critiquing currents in the sound.
Water lilies throw a feast,
For snails who're busy on their quest at least.

Life's a stream adorned with guffaws,
Each ripple giggles, each splash a cause.
So toss your worries, join the dance,
In this silly stream, take a chance!

The Followed Threads of Fate

In a world spun with laughing yarn,
A cat's paw treads on dreams unshorn,
We chase the socks that always hide,
While life winks at us with mischievous pride.

The toaster burns the bread anew,
As clocks tick sideways, how about you?
Balloons float high, yet don't seem to care,
Confetti days tossed high in the air.

A duck quacks wisdom no one knows,
Yet here we are, with silly woes,
The cereal spins, the milk goes splat,
Fate's a prankster, who can argue that?

So grab a laugh, put on your shoes,
In this grand circus, we sometimes lose,
But in the folly we find our place,
With giggles filling up the space.

Beneath the Stars, We Wonder

Under a sky that winks and glows,
We ponder life while sipping prose,
A squirrel debates at the moonlit bar,
While we count dreams like shooting stars.

A pizza floats by, just out of reach,
While planets giggle, out of our speech,
We ponder if ants have life figured right,
As we dance with shadows through the night.

Crickets chirp a confused tune,
While we debate the cheese on the moon,
And as clouds put on their nightly show,
We let our curious minds overflow.

For beneath this endless sky so vast,
We laugh at questions that never last,
In the joyful chaos of the cosmic play,
We find our way, come what may.

Tides of Time and Timelessness

The clock's hands trip in a silly dance,
Tick-tock, it teases, life's a chance,
We build sandcastles that melt in the sun,
As waves of giggles crash, we run.

The seagulls squawk like they own the beach,
While sand slips through our grasp, out of reach,
Time raises eyebrows with every surprise,
As the universe chuckles, oh so wise.

A child chases waves that never retreat,
While jellyfish swim with fluffy feet,
And as the tide takes all with a grin,
We're reminded of the silliness within.

So let's splash in puddles, dance in the rain,
Count the moments and not the mundane,
For through this jester's game of the ages,
We write our story on unwritten pages.

The Ink That Never Dries

In a world where pens just refuse to stop,
Ideas bubble over, like soda pop,
We scribble nonsense in vibrant hues,
While lazy cats plot on their dues.

The pages dance with a whimsical tune,
As the ink spills secrets beneath the moon,
Crazy drawings of dragons and cake,
In a universe where laughter's the stake.

Words tumble forth like marbles down stairs,
Prompting us to write unanswerable prayers,
While pencils doodle their thoughts on the fly,
Cracking jokes that make the erasers sigh.

So let's unravel this charming mess,
Ink may never dry, but we'll still impress,
With laughter wrapped in the paper's embrace,
We celebrate the silly, our favorite space.

Peculiar Patterns in the Chaos

In a world that spins and twirls,
Pigeons strut as if they're pearls,
The socks are lost, my keys have flown,
I laugh at things I can't condone.

When life throws curves and banana peels,
I roll with it as fate reveals,
The coffee spills, it's quite a show,
I ponder why, then let it go.

Umbrellas flip and kites collide,
While squirrels mock, and ducks decide,
I sketch a map of lost pursuits,
In puns, I find my funny roots.

So here's to chaos, absurd yet grand,
It tickles funny bones just as planned,
In this twisted dance, I sway and sway,
With a wink, I shout, "Let's play all day!"

The Song of a Silent Soliloquy

In rooms of chatter, I stand alone,
Miming thoughts with a silly tone,
The cat gives me a quizzical stare,
As I debate my imaginary hair.

Coffee cups whisper secrets low,
As I ponder how cheese can glow,
Tangled thoughts in a woolly knit,
I chuckle softly, should I commit?

Mirror reflections dance for me,
I ask the fish, "Could you agree?"
The goldfish nods, a fishy grinning,
In this game of musings, I'm always winning.

So sing with me, in sardonic glee,
Life's oddities are the key,
With every quirk that comes my way,
I'll hum a tune and laugh all day!

Chase the Echoes of Lost Moments

Chasing echoes in a hall of jest,
Where laughter plays, and we're all blessed,
I trip on memories, like worn-out shoes,
Life's circus, I muse, is full of blues.

The clock spins backward, what a sight,
Dancing shadows waltz with delight,
Each tick a riddle, each tock a grin,
I puzzle it out, where have I been?

Lost journals whisper tales to the wind,
Of half-baked plans and where I've sinned,
But with every blink, I find the cheer,
For in this mess, I've nothing to fear.

So let me chase these fleeting dreams,
With giggles big and silly schemes,
In the game of time, I'm on my toes,
With echoes laughing, anything goes!

The Weight of Seasons Unforgiven

Seasons change like a wardrobe tossed,
One minute summer, next winter frost,
I'll wear my parka with sandals too,
While dancing 'round and feeling blue.

Leaves fall down like misfired confetti,
The sky is gray, and oh so petty,
I find a snowman dressed in a tie,
Who's sipping cocoa, oh me, oh my!

Time's a joke, and I'm the clown,
With rubber boots in a golden gown,
I juggle pumpkins and red balloons,
And serenade the howling tunes.

So here's to seasons, these merry fools,
With laughter echoing, breaking the rules,
In this weighty game, I'll revel and spin,
For even chaos knows how to grin!

Ocean of Forgotten Questions

Why do socks disappear in the wash?
They swim away on a spin cycle,
Caught in currents of fabric softener,
While we're left wondering how to match.

The keys hide when you need them most,
Under the couch or inside a shoe,
A treasure hunt for the absent mate,
Who knew keys loved to play hide and seek?

Is there a ghost in the fridge at night?
Chilling leftovers, they whisper tales,
Of the time they almost turned to soup,
But chose instead to chill on the shelf.

And what of our phones, so smart and sly?
They buzz and beep while we dance along,
Yet help us locate our missing minds,
Or point us to where we left our laughs.

The Etchings of Impermanence

Life's a comedy, that's plain to see,
With punchlines missing and jokes ajar,
Like gum on a shoe, it sticks to you,
Yet leaves you laughing under the stars.

Yesterday's news, a crumpled sheet,
Makes a perfect origami crane,
Who knew that paper could fly so high,
While we debate if it's really a plane?

Time tick-tocks on a wobbly wall,
With clock hands that dance out of sync,
Like two left feet at a wedding ball,
Is it a waltz or a frantic blink?

Our memories fade like a cheap tattoo,
Though in a moment, they sparkle bright,
We laugh at the things we used to fret,
And cheer for the chaos of life's delight.

Conversations with the Subconscious

My dreams are a circus, wild and loud,
Where elephants paint and monkeys sing,
The ringmaster's lost in a trench coat,
Offering popcorn with flying wings.

Last night a cat held a board meeting,
Dressed in a tie, sipping on tea,
Discussing the matter of world domination,
While I just wanted to skip to decree.

There's wisdom in waffles and syrup's glide,
Speaking softly in the morning light,
Each bite a verse, a secret code,
That giggles when life feels too tight.

So I ask the shadows what's the deal,
With riddles wrapped in my duvet dreams,
They shrugged and danced, tap shoes on tiles,
Leaving me to ponder, or so it seems.

Navigating the Unseen

We're sailing seas of tangled thoughts,
With maps drawn by lost roller skates,
Navigating quirks with a spoonful of laughs,
In this buffet of curious fates.

What's that noise? A crumpet speaking?
Or perhaps the fridge is plotting a coup,
With leftovers marching like tiny troops,
Declaring "we won't rot, we'll stick like glue!"

Shadows flutter, toss about the room,
Casting worries as we chase the breeze,
Debating the logic of socks in the sink,
As if missing fabric held the keys.

So let's toast to the absurdity we find,
In the cosmos of crumbs and coffee spills,
For every question worth its weight in time,
Has a punchline that's sure to give you thrills.

Echoes of a Forgotten Journey

We travel far, we wander wide,
With maps that lead us, yet we chide.
A quest for gold or just for fun,
But tripping over shoes, we run.

In every town, a tale is spun,
Of quests forgotten, laughs undone.
With no great plans but snacks to share,
We find our joy in the lost air.

Like clouds that drift, then disappear,
Our goals are funny, never clear.
We dance with dreams that twist and shout,
Then trip and tumble—who's knocked out?

Yet in the laughs and silly grins,
We've found the gold—where journey begins.

Wash Away the Gray

When Monday's here, it brings dismay,
We curse the clock that steals our play.
Yet coffee's magic brews delight,
It paints our world in shades so bright.

We splash in puddles, giggle loud,
While adulting wears a solemn shroud.
Life's like a canvas, smeared and gray,
But we just laugh; we wash away.

With every mishap, we take a shot,
Dancing like jesters, tying knots.
So bring the joy, erase the stress,
In silly moments, we feel blessed.

So grab a brush, let colors rule,
In each mishap, we find the jewel.

Entangled in Existence

In life's big web, we crawl and weave,
A tangled path, we laugh, believe.
With every thread that snares us tight,
We juggle chaos, it's pure delight.

Trying to adult, we often fail,
Like cats who chase a wayward tail.
Yet in the mess, there's often grace,
In goofy falls, we find our place.

Existence flings us 'round like yarn,
We laugh at trials that make us worn.
Like popcorn popping, we break free,
Embracing life's absurdity.

So here we are, both lost and found,
In silly jigs, our joy unbound.

The Canvas of a Curious Mind

With brushes wild, we paint our dreams,
Splashing colors in humorous streams.
A canvas filled with doodled lies,
As curious thoughts take to the skies.

We scribble worlds, both weird and bright,
In every goofy stroke, pure delight.
Yet logic bows to whimsy's reign,
In playful chaos, joy we gain.

Like kids with crayons, nothing's wrong,
We craft our story in silly song.
Each mark a giggle, a wobbly line,
Just like our thoughts, they twist and twine.

So grab your muse, let nonsense flow,
In the curious mind, let laughter grow.

A Silhouette Against the Setting Sun

Standing tall, a shadow plays,
Dreams of fortune in a haze.
Life's a circus, quite absurd,
Chasing tails, have you heard?

The sunset laughs, it winks at me,
Time's a thief, it loves to flee.
Juggling hope like an old clown,
Wishing for a gold crown!

Every laugh, a fleeting sigh,
Bake a pie, then let it fly.
The horizon spills its paint,
Life's a joke, but who's the saint?

So here we pose, all in jest,
Fleeting glances, we're all guests.
In this show, the stars align,
Yet still we stumble through the wine.

The Rhythm of Tired Feet

Tap, tap, tapping on the ground,
With each step, a world renowned.
Check my watch, it's way too late,
Still I juggle dreams and fate.

Shuffle here, a wiggle there,
Stomp my woes, release the air.
Dance of life with mismatched shoes,
Got a penny? Let's buy some views!

Every ache, a funny tale,
Hopping down the cosmic trail.
Feet are weary, spirits bright,
Under the disco ball of night.

With each beat, the laughter swells,
Pay your dues to the jester's bells.
Tired feet, but hearts will soar,
For every step, we crave one more!

Fragments of a Once Whole Soul

Bits and pieces on the floor,
Collecting dust, who wants much more?
Chasing shadows of my past,
Hoping each laugh will forever last.

A jigsaw puzzle, oh so nice,
Cardboard cutouts, let's roll the dice.
A smile here, a frown right there,
Building dreams on a broken chair.

Oddly shaped, yet still I shine,
Wearing mismatched socks, divine!
Life is crazy, what a ride,
In these fragments, I'll abide.

So let's toast to the crazy bits,
Raise our glasses, let's not quit.
Each small piece, a silly role,
We're all fragments of one whole soul!

Beneath the Surface of Still Waters

Ripples come with a chuckle loud,
Bubbles float, like a laughing crowd.
Fish in hats swim by with ease,
Passing notes on a gentle breeze.

Water's surface, glassy, bright,
Hiding tales under moonlight.
Each splash tells a joke or two,
What's the fish's favorite brew?

Beneath the waves, a catfish grins,
Telling jokes about his fins.
Life is fluid, never bland,
Joking rivers, laughing sand.

So dive deep, take the plunge,
With every splash, there's time to lunge.
Beneath the calm, a party reigns,
Where every giggle breaks the chains!

Tangles of Time and Emotion

In the web of life we spin,
Chasing dreams through thick and thin.
Like socks that vanish in the wash,
We laugh and cry, then start to squosh.

Moments twist, then make us grin,
Like finding out we weren't quite thin.
We juggle thoughts like clumsy clowns,
Wearing mismatched shoes and frowns.

With coffee spills and shoe lace trips,
We collect mishaps like quirky scripts.
Laughter echoes through our days,
In this tangly, goofy maze.

Yet somehow through the wild parade,
We dance on fears that often fade.
So let's embrace the silly quest,
And wear our chaos like a vest.

Reflections in a Rain-Splattered Window

Raindrops race like little cars,
On windows showing thoughts of ours.
We ponder life with coffee brews,
While watching clouds change up their hues.

The world outside, a blurry view,
Like memories that fade, it's true.
We chuckle at the messy scene,
As cats zoom past, too fast, too keen.

Umbrellas flip, with laughter shared,
Dodging puddles, slightly scared.
Each splash a joke the raindrops crack,
In this slippery, funny track.

So let the storm bring silly whims,
As we dance through life and sing our hymns.
For every drop that falls and plops,
Is just another chance for hops.

The Fleeting Flicker of a Candle

A candle flickers, a dance of light,
    Winking softly in the night.
We gather 'round with snacks galore,
    Hoping it won't dim for sure.

With every sway, the shadows play,
    Echoing thoughts of yesterday.
We laugh at wax that's dripped and oozed,
    While trying hard not to get snoozed.

Each flicker brings an awkward quirk,
    As if the flame has gone to work.
We ponder life's mysterious blend,
With every flick, there's bliss to mend.

So grab a snack and toast the scene,
As candles dance like a quirky dream.
In life's brief glow, may joy abound,
    With laughter's spark forever found.

A Garden of Unanswered Questions

In a garden where odd thoughts bloom,
We ask the stars about their room.
Why do socks seem to go astray?
And where's the end of every day?

Bees buzz by with a hasty drone,
While wondering if they're really known.
Is the grass greener or just a tease?
With every breeze, our worries freeze.

We plant our doubts like seeds in rows,
Hoping to see how each one grows.
But life hangs curtains on its quest,
Leaving us pondering without rest.

So let's embrace this silly field,
Where laughter's fruit is freely yield.
As questions swirl like dancing leaves,
In this quirky garden, time believes.

The Silence of Inquiry

Why do we ponder the stars so high?
Do they wonder if we ask or cry?
A cat on the roof, stares up with a blink,
What do they know? Now that makes us think!

We scribble our notes, in margins we scrawl,
As if in the cosmos, we're making a call.
With coffee in hand, we sip and we sigh,
Maybe it's cosmic, or maybe just pie!

The universe laughs, with a hilarious plunk,
As we chase our own tails, like a puppy in junk.
With each question tossed, like confetti in air,
The answer's a mystery, but who even cares?

So here we are lost, in a cocktail of thought,
Is the joke on us? Or are we all caught?
Raise a glass to the musings, let laughter ignite,
For in this vast chaos, we just might feel light!

Beneath the Surface of Everyday

In a world of routine, we shuffle and glide,
But beneath the surface, there's a wild tide.
Coffee spills over, a mug full of dreams,
While socks in the dryer plan schemes and teams.

Toasters conspire, they burn just for fun,
As we chase after crumbs, on a quest 'til we're done.
Each trip to the fridge is a journey anew,
The dance of a snack, should we savor or stew?

Beneath quiet sidewalks, the ants have a race,
Plot twists in the parking lot, all at your pace.
The mundane's a playground for joy to reveal,
With laughter and mishaps, it's a merry meal!

So let's embrace chaos, in traffic or play,
Find humor in nothing, let laughter lead the way.
Each day may seem simple, yet splendidly vast,
In the ordinary odd, let our fun be cast!

An Odyssey in Stillness

In a room of calm, a sock starts to dance,
While the chair hums a tune, in a whimsical trance.
A spider spins tales, 'bout the bugs of the day,
While cushions conspire to lead us astray.

The clock on the wall, it mocks with a tick,
Count your missed minutes, that's the real trick!
As we ponder our fate, on chairs we repose,
Life may take flight, oh where did it go?

With popcorn for thought, in front of the screen,
Is the couch really sinking? Or are we just lean?
Each moment a snapshot, in laughter we pause,
Navigating life's maze, without many laws.

So let's find the joy, in quietest times,
In each silent giggle, through life's pantomimes.
For in an odyssey slow, we might find a clue,
That life's grand adventure is often just you!

The Enigma of Fleeting Time

Time's a peculiar chap, dressed in a coat,
He laughs as he tickles the hour, afloat.
While we count our minutes, like sheep on a run,
He's out there dancing, having all the fun!

With calendars tangled, in knots and in twirls,
We lose track of days, like lost little pearls.
As we try to catch time, it's like herding cats,
He slips through our fingers, how does he do that?

Each second a whisper, that teases and teases,
Just when we think we've caught it, it sneezes!
So we sit with our clocks, and grumble some more,
In the race of the ages, we're keeping the score.

But let's not forget, within these mad rhymes,
There's laughter to pluck, amidst ticking chimes.
For time is a trickster, delightfully sly,
In the enigma of seconds, let humor fly high!

Threads of Light in the Darkness

In the deep of night, I saw a spark,
A glow so bright, it left a mark.
Tangled webs of weird delight,
I laughed at shadows, dancing light.

Why chase the stars when I can trip,
Over socks and coffee sip?
Life's a thread, so rough yet fine,
I wear it well, it suits my line.

A cat meows with utmost flair,
As if to say, 'Do you even care?'
I nod and shrug, my head is spun,
From all the shiny, pointless fun.

So here's to chaos, a toast to fate,
I juggle nonsense, it's never late.
In this odd circus, I hold my breath,
Finding joy in the dance of death.

The Pulse of a Restless Dreamer

Chasing dreams like a squirrel in flight,
I trip on clouds, oh what a sight!
Doodles and wishes, scribbled grace,
With coffee spills all over my face.

I wander through aisles of cosmic snacks,
Counting the stars before they relax.
A tick-tock melody pounds in my chest,
Running in circles, I'll never rest.

The sun yawns wide, birds flip a coin,
To see who wins the morning adjoin.
Life's a party, can't you see?
Where chaos reigns and dreams run free.

A wild dance on a wobbly floor,
I twirl and leap, shout, "Give me more!"
Each fractured moment isn't quite right,
But I'm still laughing, and that's my flight.

Glistening Drops of Ephemeral Time

Tickling seconds like dew on grass,
I sip my tea as minutes pass.
A world of wonder, oh so bright,
Yet time spills out like soggy light.

Moments flop like a fish on land,
Each one worth less than a rubber band.
I catch the laughter, let it flow,
Like sparkles bouncing in sun's glow.

With every tick, the clock will grumble,
As I skip down paths of humble jumble.
Living life like a stick of gum,
Chewy and wild, it's never glum.

So here's my toast to droplet days,
Each one a dance in strange ballet.
Though fleeting may be every gust,
I collect the smiles and treasure the rust.

eDancing on the Edge of Certainty

Balancing thoughts like a tightrope act,
With tippy toes and a wobbly snack.
I twirl my doubts into silly hats,
Embracing the unknown like curious cats.

Each question bounces, a spring-loaded toy,
As answers giggle and try to annoy.
I'm spinning maps of confounding streets,
Where the lost and found have crazy beats.

A riddle of life, a puzzle to solve,
With pieces missing and no resolve.
Yet in the chaos, I find my song,
In the dance of doubt, I still belong.

So let me waltz on this shaky line,
With whimsy as my partner, how divine!
The edge may tremble, but I'll take the ride,
With laughter and grace, it's my wild slide.

Silent Yearnings Beneath the Stars

In the night we gaze and sigh,
Thinking what if pigs can fly.
Stars above, they wink and tease,
As we ponder life's big cheese.

Uncle Joe with his grand scheme,
Trying to bake a moonlit dream.
But the cake just fell flat, oh dear,
Now he's chasing shadows, I fear.

Glimmers of hope in the dark sky,
Maybe it's best to bake a pie.
With laughter shared and crumbs to spill,
Life's sweet taste, a laughter thrill.

So let's count stars and laugh out loud,
Join the dance, be silly, be proud.
For in the cosmic jest we find,
The universe has a funny mind.

Pondering the Silk of Infinity

In echoes of a pondered thought,
Like tangled yarn from a cat we've caught.
Infinity swirls, wears a funny hat,
As we trip on questions, where's the mat?

A very wise man once did say,
Life's a game, come what may.
He then fell into a tub of goo,
Maybe he knew something we didn't too!

With swirling galaxies, donuts in space,
Each sunrise an absurd embrace.
At cosmic cafés we sip on whimsy,
Sharing chuckles, oh so flimsy.

Though the answers hide like shy mice,
We'll dance through the questions, oh so nice.
For the silk of infinity's quite a riddle,
Let's hum and laugh, and play the fiddle.

The Allure of the Abyss

Peering down into the deep,
Where lurking thoughts seem to creep.
Is that a fish or just a shoe?
Maybe it's life, waiting for you!

Abyss with secrets dark and grand,
What's lurking there? A marching band?
They play a tune, it's all quite absurd,
While above we're lost for words!

Dive in deep, let's take a peek,
Perhaps the void has some wisdom to leak.
With giggles bouncing, we float and glide,
In the allure, we'll take the ride.

So toss your worries like an old shoe,
In the depths, we'll laugh 'til we're blue.
For in the unknown, a joy persists,
The abyss just can't resist.

A Riddle Wrapped in Silence

In the quiet depths, a riddle lies,
Like a cat with its cunning eyes.
What's hidden there? A marshmallow?
Does that mean we should just follow?

Chasing whispers, we trip on air,
Floating in thoughts, without a care.
Do we giggle, or is that a sneeze?
Perhaps it's just life's silly tease.

Wrapped in silence, the mystery spins,
Could it be where the sock thief grins?
Tickled by questions that tease and poke,
In this riddle, let laughter evoke.

So gather 'round with friends so dear,
Share a chuckle, bring the cheer.
For in the silence, we'll find the jest,
Turns out laughter's simply the best!

Reflections in a Foggy Mirror

I look at my face, who is that guy?
With hair like a cloud and a very dry eye.
The mirror's all fogged, oh what a delight,
Is this how I'll look on my next birthday night?

The toothpaste is specked, my shirt has a stain,
I laugh at the chaos, forget all the pain.
With grace like a swan and the charm of a dog,
Maybe being absurd is the path through the fog.

A dance of reflections, all jumbled and skewed,
I'll take a big sip from my cup of brewed.
If life is a puzzle, I've lost a few pieces,
But who needs them all when the laughter increases?

So here's to the madness, let's twirl in the haze,
To finding a smile on the fog's steamy phase.
Life's just a jest with a pie in the face,
We'll frolic in nonsense; oh, what a great place!

The Labyrinth of Uncertainty

A maze without clues, where do I turn?
The walls made of questions, and still I learn.
With each twist and a shout, I meet the odd,
Maybe I'm just a pawn in a cosmic plod.

I trip on my thoughts, like shoes on a string,
Is that a wise owl or an old rubber spring?
The path seems so wobbly, I may well be wrong,
But I'll skip and I'll hop, that's how I stay strong.

A rabbit or tortoise, who really knows?
The finish line's elusive, nobody shows.
I laugh as I wander through this curious game,
As life adds a twist, just to keep it all lame.

So toss out the map; I prefer the surprise,
Let's dance with the chaos, let laughter arise.
In this grand maze of mishaps, I'll twirl, I'll prance,
For stumbling through life is its own sort of chance!

A Tapestry of Unfulfilled Dreams

I wove a fine dream with colors so bright,
But snagged on reality, it gave me a fright.
The threads fell apart, in a tangle and mess,
Yet here I am laughing, still feeling quite blessed.

With visions of grandeur, I planned a grand feast,
But ended up munching on crackers, at least.
The soufflé I whipped turned to pancake-like goo,
But I served it with pride, yeah, it's something to chew!

A castle in Spain? Oh, what a fine sight!
But I'm stuck in my room, in my pajamas tonight.
I'll strut like a peacock in dreams yet deferred,
For life's a wild jest, and laughter's preferred.

So here's to the dreams that flutter and sway,
They guide me through nights and bright up my day.
With a chuckle or two, I'll keep spinning my thread,
For a tapestry rich is the laughter we spread!

Sifting Through Dust

I sift through the dust of my yesterdays lost,
Hoping to find that raw sugar at cost.
But all I uncover are crumbs of regret,
And a sock without partners, oh what a duet!

Old gadgets and trinkets, each with a tale,
Of battles with boredom or saga to trail.
The memories linger, like crumbs on my face,
Turns out I was born for an odd sort of race.

With laughter in hand, I'll sweep up the floor,
In search of a sandwich or maybe just more.
The treasures I seek may just quirkily blend,
For sifting through dust is a method to mend.

So here's to the clutter, the chaos, the fun,
Distractions that bring joy when the day is all done.
I'll shine up the corners, let laughter combust,
For each hidden treasure is worth all the dust!

Unfolding the Paradox of Being

Life's a riddle, oh so tight,
We dance in circles, day and night.
With every question, more to find,
A punchline hidden, quite unkind.

Wake up, get dressed, then hit the ground,
Chasing our tails, look around.
But in this chaos, laughter's found,
Amidst the folly, joy's profound.

Coffee spills and socks gone missing,
Every mishap has its kissing.
In life's circus, we wear our masks,
Giggles bubble up from mundane tasks.

So let us twirl, both bold and brave,
In life's mad plot, we'll misbehave.
For in this jest, the truth may gleam,
A cosmic laugh, a silly dream.

Lost in the Pages of Yesterday

Flip the book, where did we land?
With coffee stains and a trembling hand.
Echoes of laughter, whispers of glee,
A plot twist waiting, can't you see?

Time's a page-turner, dog-eared and worn,
We chase the shadows, blissfully scorn.
Memories dance like confetti in air,
But we trip on nostalgia, unaware.

Once I was wise, or so I claimed,
Now I'm a joker, slightly ashamed.
Pages of foolery fill up my plot,
Writing new verses, forgetting the dot.

Yet here I am, pen in hand,
Crafting a tale that feels so bland.
But the laughter spills, like ink on the floor,
In this wild tale, I'm always wanting more.

Paths Woven in the Dark

Stumbling forward, who needs a guide?
In the shadows, our giggles hide.
Step on a crack, break your mom's back,
Or was it a fortune lost in the sack?

We weave through nights, like socks on the floor,
Each twist and turn, can't keep score.
Found a way out? Or are we just lost?
Not all who wander pay the cost.

Moonlight chuckles, the stars all agree,
In this maze, we're all slightly free.
Let's hop on a whim, skip to the beat,
Tripping on dreams, we can't face defeat.

So if you stumble, just laugh it out,
Life's comic timing is what it's about.
For every misstep, there's joy to savor,
In the dark paths, find your own flavor.

The Silence Between Words

Caught in the pauses, giggles await,
Between the lines, we negotiate fate.
A wink, a nod, the jesters we are,
Bantering nonsense on life's little star.

Chatterboxes bound with tape on our lips,
Yet silence ripples, laughter it strips.
Between every sigh, a joke unfolds,
In stillness, the heart's comedy molds.

Breathe in the quiet, let humor arise,
In the space of silence, winks turn to sighs.
Fumbles of chatter, a comedy show,
Where whispers of mirth and madness flow.

So here we stand, in a pause so sweet,
Life's punchline hidden in quiet conceit.
Laugh at the hush, embrace the absurd,
For joy often dances without a word.

Whispers of a Wandering Heart

A cat on a roof with a grand view,
Pondering life with a good stretch or two.
Why chase the mice, what's the cost?
When napping is clearly the life that's not lost.

Butterflies giggle, the grass makes a tease,
As squirrels hold meetings beneath shady trees.
Does playing all day make the sunset more sweet?
Or is boredom the prize for our busy little feet?

A Question Mark in the Sky

Up in the clouds, a balloon floats away,
Holding secrets of all we don't say.
Do the stars laugh when we trip on our shoes?
Or does the moon wink at our humorous blues?

A dog with a stick thinks he's quite profound,
While the winds of change swirl all around.
Is the journey more fun than the destination's thrill?
Or is running in circles just part of the drill?

Dandelion Dreams and Empty Pages

A dandelion puffs, spreading wishes like seeds,
While scribbles of life plant peculiar needs.
Why do we ponder while balancing spoons?
Could it be better in twinkling, jolly tunes?

A paper plane sails, with a flip and a whirl,
Chasing the clouds in a wobbly swirl.
Do dreams change direction with each passing hour?
Or just take a nap in a patch of fresh flowers?

The Weight of Unspoken Thoughts

A turtle with wisdom moves slow down the lane,
While frogs in the pond dance in the rain.
Do whispers of silence drown out the loud?
Or do we just giggle and feel a bit proud?

A fish in a bowl thinks he's quite wise,
Telling tales of the world in his colorful guise.
But who needs deep thoughts on a swing in the park?
When laughter is bright and ignites even sparks?

Echoes of Silent Inquiry

Why do we chase the clock's hands,
When time's just a house of cards?
We laugh and we fumble, like clumsy bands,
Yet nobody's keeping score for our regards.

The coffee spills, a wake-up call,
As crumbs dance from last night's feast.
We wonder if we matter at all,
While debating the merits of toast and yeast.

In meetings where gibberish reigns,
We wave around our witty shields.
Do puns make us wise, or just plain drains?
Half-baked ideas in brainstorming fields.

So let's rejoice in our quest for the jest,
For life's grand ballet is quite the scene.
With chuckles and giggles, we'll settle the quest,
As we narrowly dodge the routine routine.

Searching for Meaning in Shadows

Dancing with shadows, we trip on the lines,
While pondering if socks have sentience.
The cat stares at us, as if it divines,
That losing the remote should require repentance.

We search for the gold beyond life's gray veil,
While fries in the fridge debate their own worth.
If fries could talk, would they sing or wail?
And what if the cosmos is just a big mirth?

Peeking through curtains, we play hide-and-seek,
With hopes that might float like a styrofoam boat.
But life's not a game, and no one's unique,
As we follow our hearts like a timid goat.

Laughter erupts as we sip from our cups,
Shadows may whisper, but we'll never mend.
To ask simple questions, like silly grown-ups,
Leads us to wisdom, but never to end.

A Canvas of Doubt

I paint with confusion, splashes of cheer,
As brushes collide, a colorful mess.
Are we artists or clowns, facing our fear?
With a palette of giggles that we can't suppress.

The canvas unfolds, a spectacle vast,
While masterpieces blend with our flops.
Each stroke holds a question that's destined to last,
Like socks that go missing and never swap shops.

We splatter our whims, and suddenly freeze,
Is this art or just chaos in motion?
Collectors of moments, we aim to please,
But find ourselves lost in the sea of emotion.

Yet laughter erupts from this muddled affair,
As paint drips from brushes like tears from the sun.
In this funny circus of colors laid bare,
We're artists of life, and we're all having fun.

The Puzzle with Missing Pieces

A jigsaw of life with a corner gone rogue,
The pieces are laughing, they've mismatched again.
We search for the edge like a whimsical bog,
While pondering where all the socks went then.

With colors that clash and shapes that confound,
It seems the cat's played a game with my heart.
Edges of feeling obscurely renowned,
As I wrestle with fragments that form my own art.

At times I feel like I'm missing my odds,
Each fitting attempt a delightful charade.
Laughter escapes as we ponder the gods,
Who've surely misplaced the last piece I made.

So pass me a piece or a slice of your cheer,
Let's chuckle together at this puzzling spree.
With giggles and gaffes, we'll conquer our fear,
For life's just a puzzle; let's set our minds free.

www.ingramcontent.com/pod-product-compliance
Lightning Source LLC
Chambersburg PA
CBHW051658160426
43209CB00004B/947